To:

From:

MOM, I LOVE YOU

101 Reasons Why

LovityNote
Mom, I Love You

www.lovitynote.com

First published by LovityNote in Germany in 2022
First printed April 2022

9783949676048

First Edition

Dear Mom,

I wrote this book about you, and this is my way of showing you my love and appreciation. In this book, you'll find all the heartfelt details of our unique relationship, written in words of gratitude to thank you for being the best mom I could ever ask for. Navigate through this journal's pages to find all the little treasures I keep safe for you. Happy reading!

Lots of love,

____

1

You are the first person I want to

....

when

....

2

Your superpower is

....

3

Thanks to you, I've become more

....

and less

....

4

The best advice you've ever given me is

....

5

Your

....

is what I miss the most when you're away.

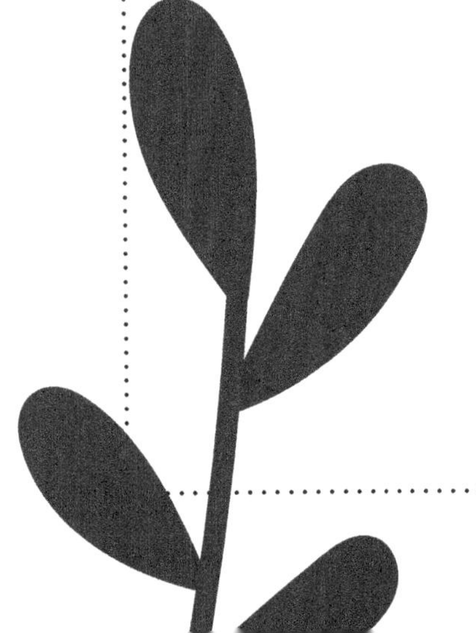

6

I always feel special and loved when you

....

7

No one can cook

better than you.

8

The best gift I've
received from you is

....

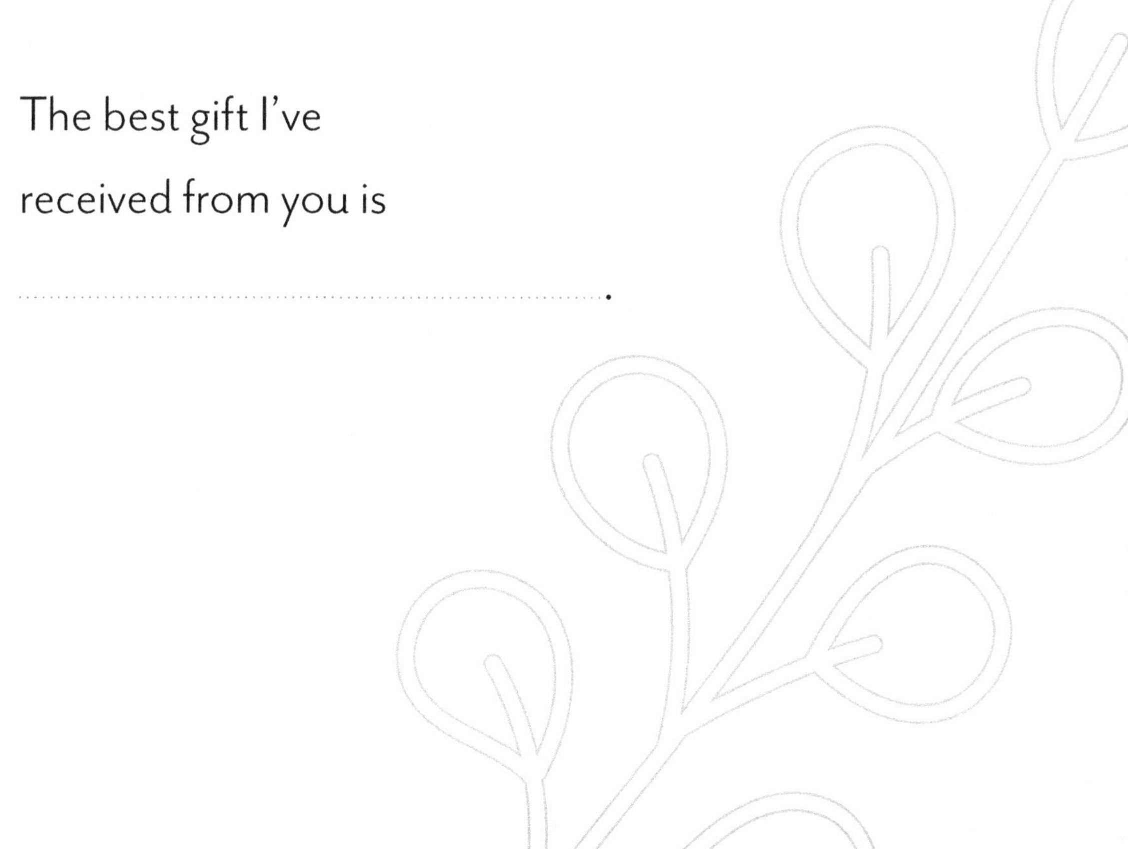

9

You encourage me to

....

even when

....

10

The top three qualities that I'm proud to have inherited from you are:

1. ....

2. ....

3. ....

11

You are a great role model for

....

because

....

12

You inspire me to

....

Your love of

....

has helped me appreciate

....

14

My favorite travel memory with you is

....

15

Somehow you always seem to

....,

and that makes me feel

....

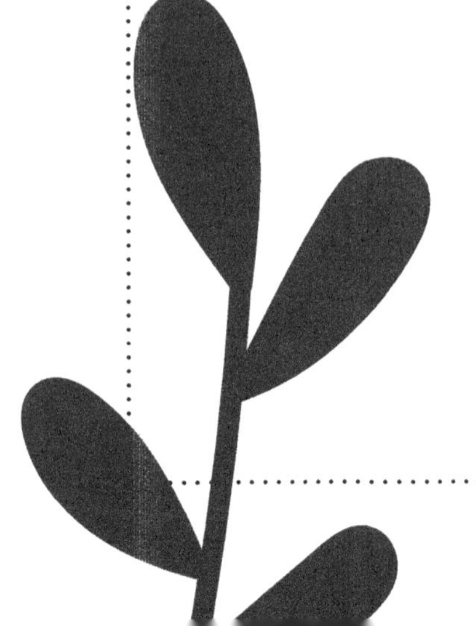

16

I've always admired the way you

....

17

Your greatest talent is

....

18

I'll always remember the time you surprised me with

....

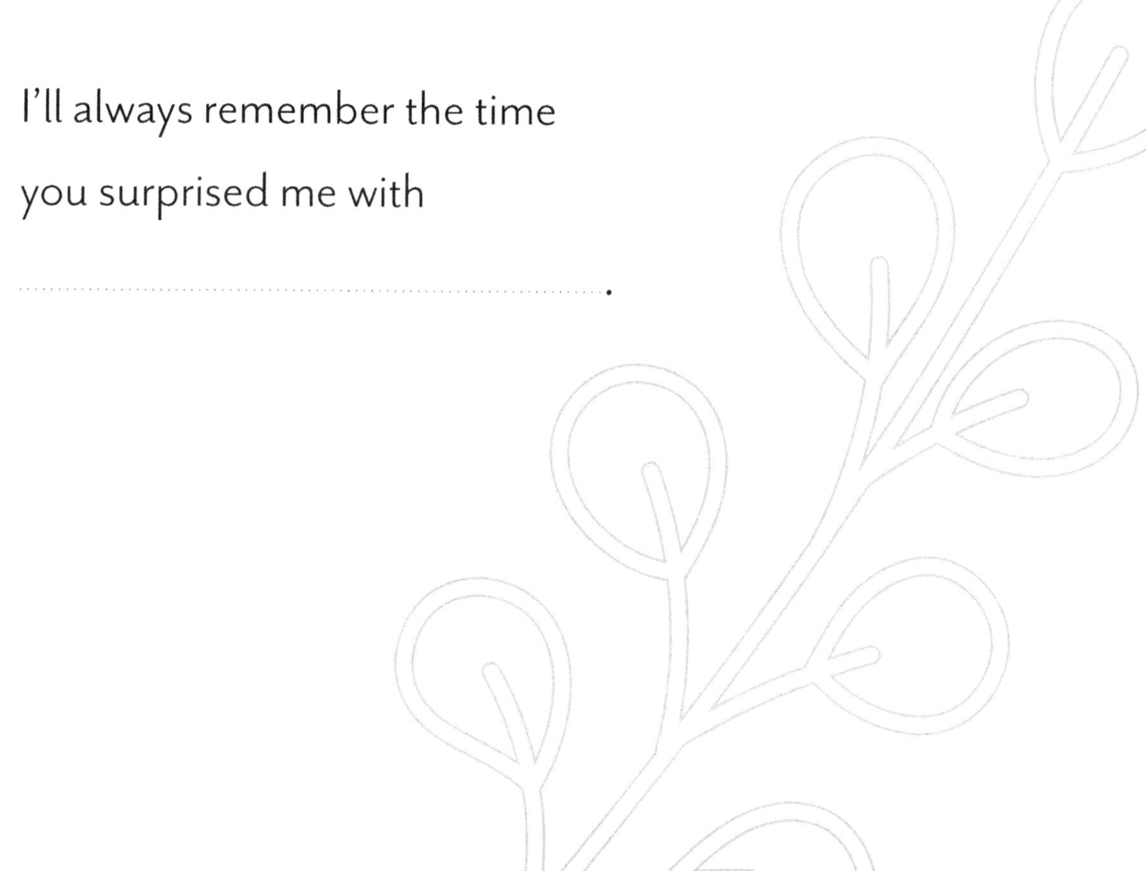

19

I love that you care so much about

....

20

Being a mom isn't easy, and I'm amazed by how well you manage to

....

21

I particularly enjoy going

....

with you because

....

22

I look up to you because

....

I wouldn't be able to

....

if you hadn't shown me the way.

24

The funniest conversation we've ever had was

....

25

I like recalling the nicest thing I've ever heard you say about me, and that's

………………………………………………………………………….

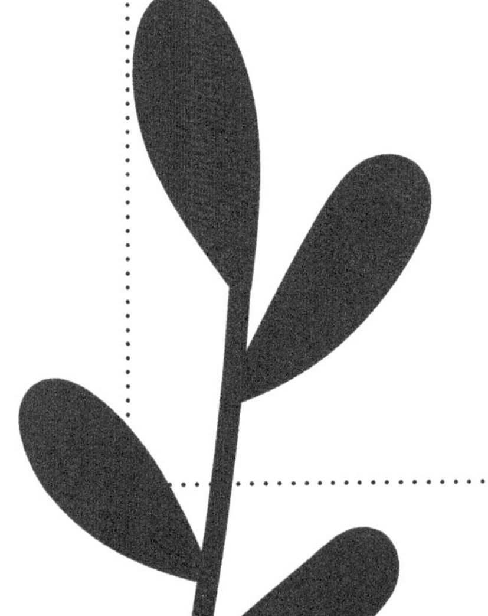

26

I always feel comforted when you

....

27

You love me in times when

....

28

You always manage to cheer me up when you

....

29

You deserve

....

because

....

30

The top three things you do that annoy me but make you a great mom are:

1. ....

2. ....

3. ....

31

One thing I get to appreciate more about you with each passing day is

....

32

You have great taste in

....

We've shared countless happy moments together, but if I had to highlight one, it would probably be

....

34

I love that I can talk to you about

....

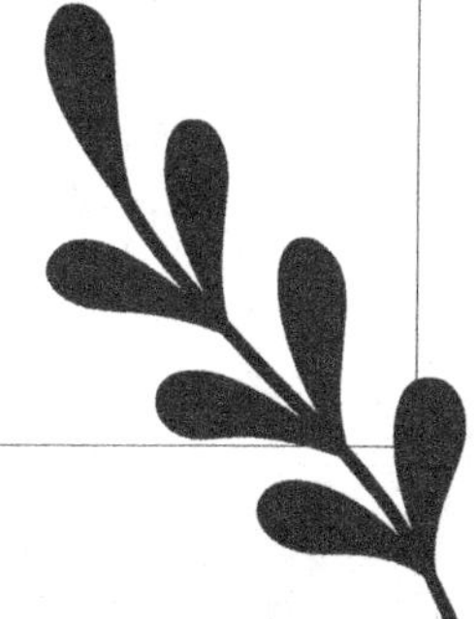

35

One thing most people don't know about you is

....

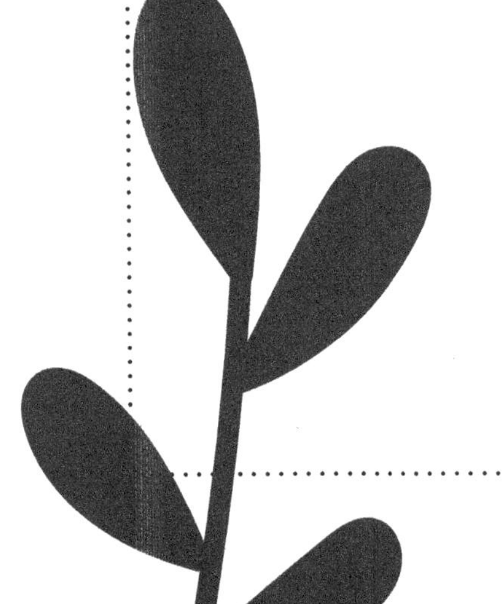

36

You are so good at

....

37

I always trust your opinion when it comes to

....

38

My favorite way of being pampered by you is

....

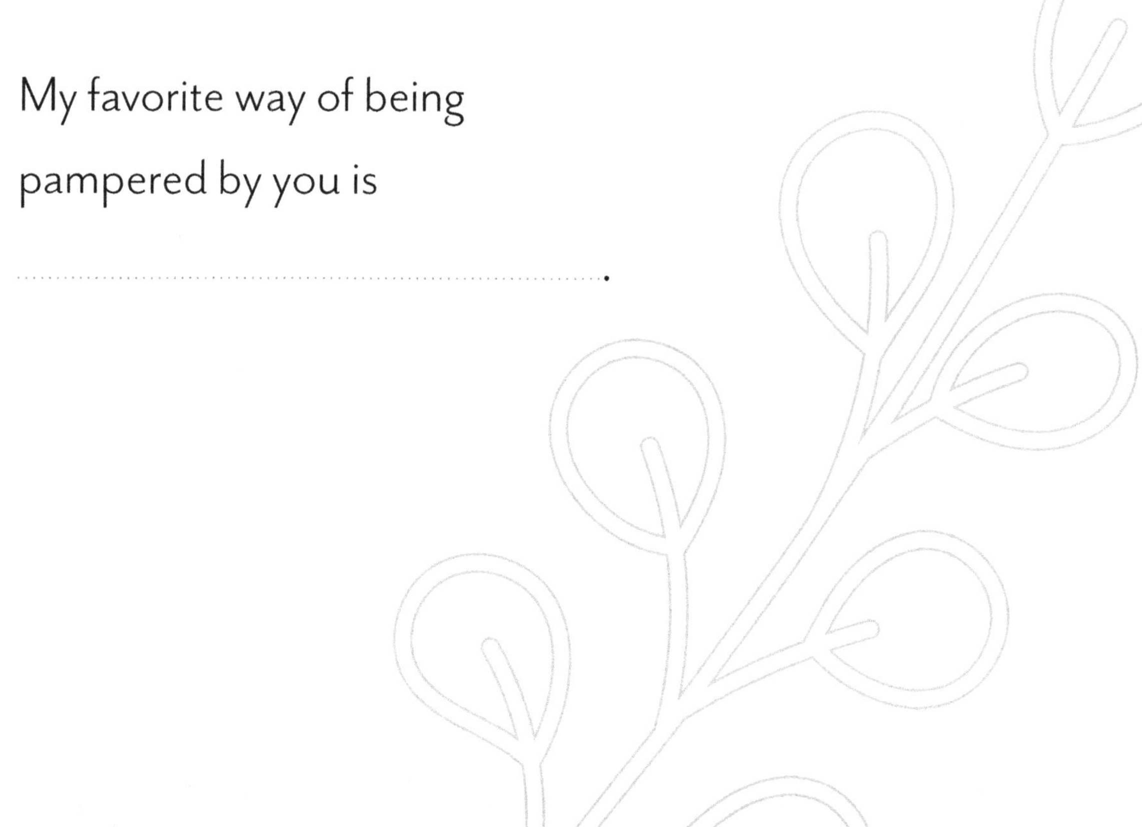

39

We both love

....,

and that's why

....

40

The top three values you've instilled in me are:

1. ....

2. ....

3. ....

41

You are the only person

who can make me

....

42

You make the best

....

I love that you always put

....

first even when

....

44

I'll be forever grateful to you for

....

45

It's wonderful that

brings us the same pleasure and joy.

46

You always impress me with

....

47

I love that you always

....

no matter what.

48

I'll never forget that you kept your promise to

....

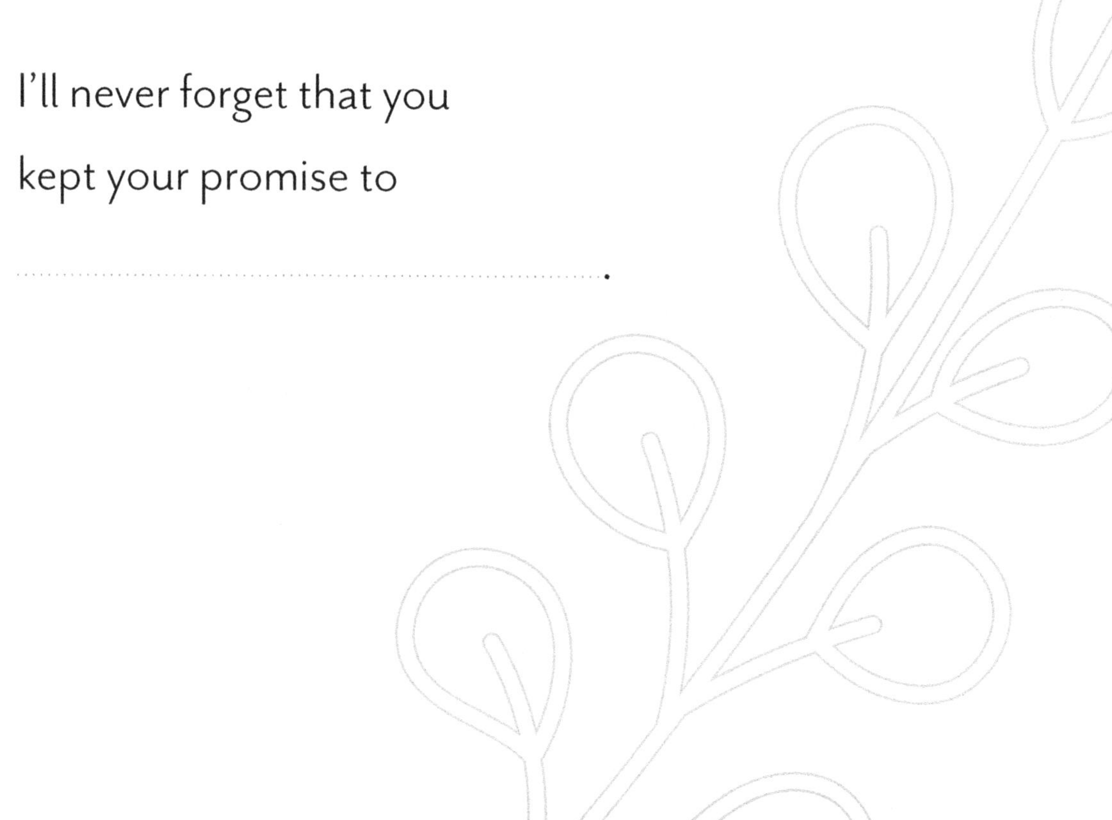

49

My favorite way that you show me affection is

....

50

It's always heartwarming to remember the time when we

....

....

51

I’m truly sorry for all the times you had to put up with my

....

52

It excites me how passionate you are about

....

I like the way you talk about me
whenever you refer to

....

54

I've always been secretly jealous of your

....

55

We usually make an awesome duo, but we would be laughably bad if we ever tried to

....

together.

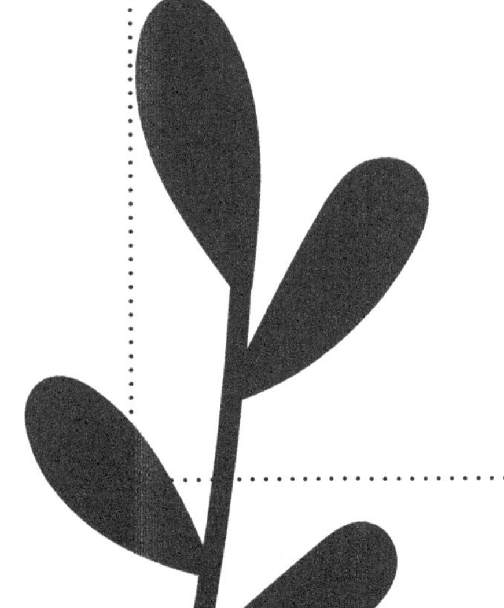

56

Thank you for all the times you

....

57

The moment I felt the proudest to be your child was

…………………………………………………………….

58

I love it when you affectionately call me

....

59

I appreciate that you always

....

to make me feel

....**.**

60

Something that I'd rather do with you out of all the people I know is

....

61

You remind me of

....

because

....

62

My sweetest memory of you is

63

I appreciate how willingly you

....

even though I know you do
it just to make me happy.

64

The top three reasons you deserve the World's Best Mom award are:

1. ....

2. ....

3. ....

65

The time when you

....

always makes me laugh.

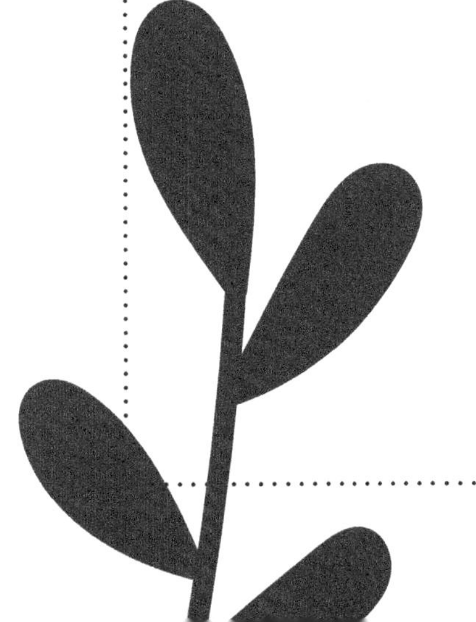

66

You've helped me overcome my fear of

....

67

I'll never forget when you saved the day by

....

....

68

Your greatest stories
revolve around

....

69

I know that you love and care for me simply because

....

70

If you were a flower, you would be a

....

because you're

....

and

....

71

I'll never forget how

....

I felt when you

....

72

My favorite adventure with you is

....

You are the reason that I have learned so much about

....

74

The three most important things that you've taught me are:

1. ....

2. ....

3. ....

75

My all-time favorite photo of us is

because

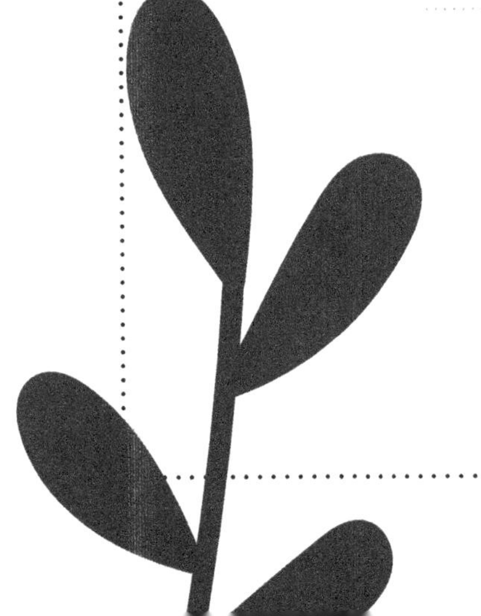

76

My favorite holiday memory with you is

....

....

77

You were so proud of me when I

……………………………………………………….

78

You've given me the confidence I need to

....

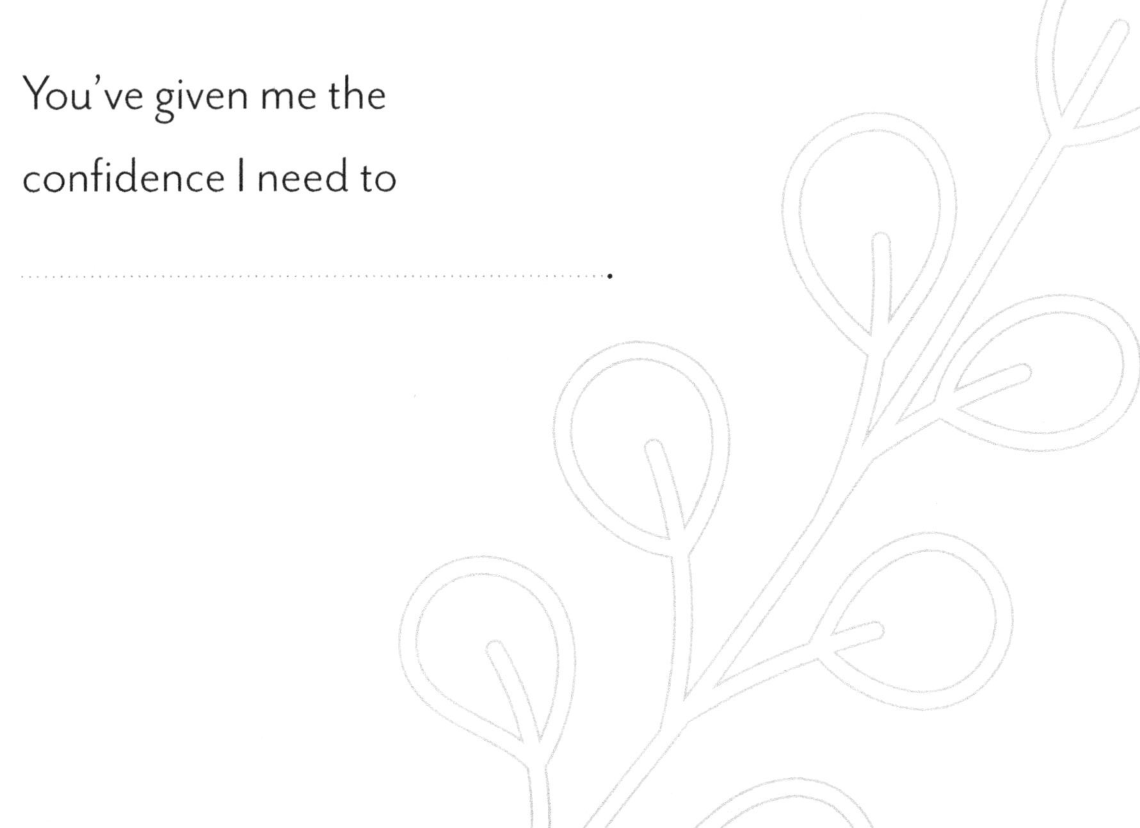

79

You are the only person I feel comfortable knowing my secret about

....

80

The three most precious non-material things that you've given me are:

1. ....

2. ....

3. ....

81

You are the only person

I know who can

....

82

I admire your dedication to

....

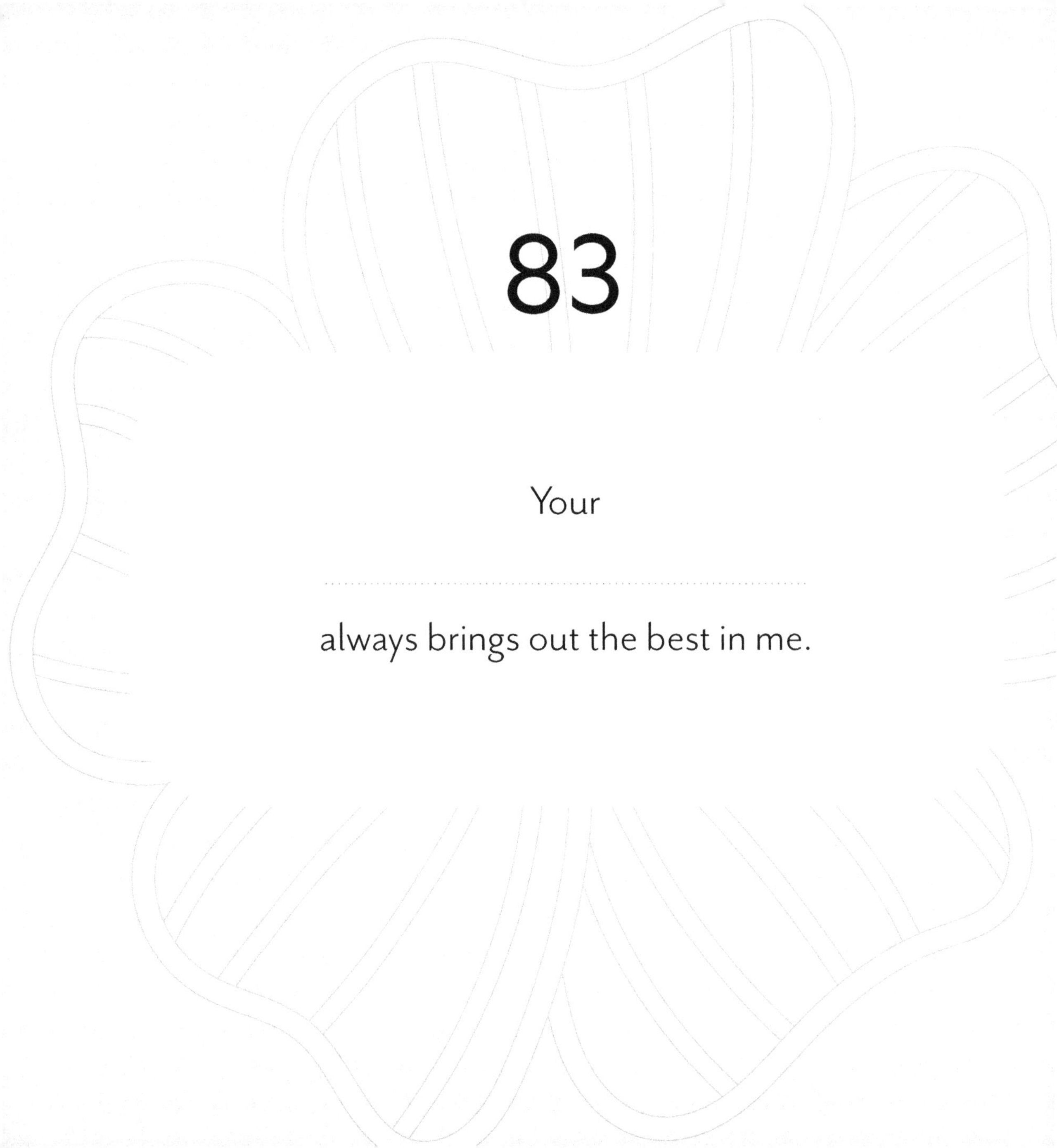

83

Your

....

always brings out the best in me.

84

The day you

....

holds a special place in my heart.

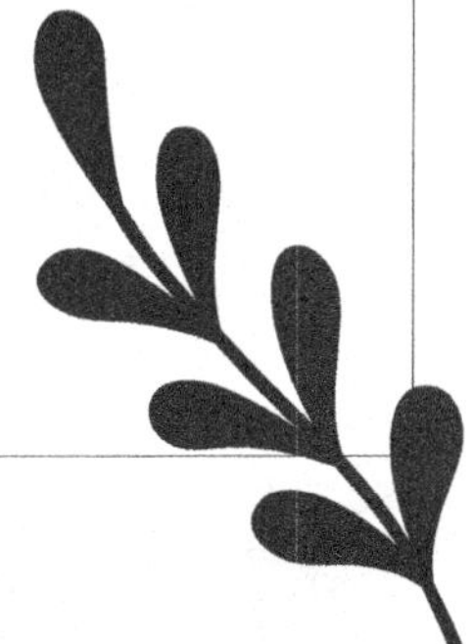

85

You always make sure I

....,

and I'm thankful for that.

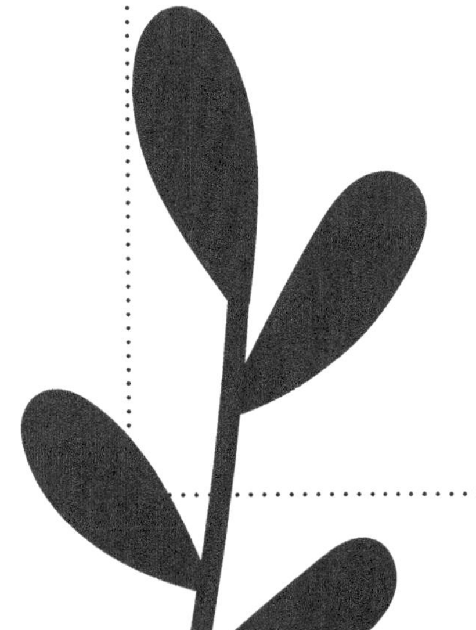

86

One of your quirks that I love about you is

....

87

You accept my

....

and make me feel less imperfect.

88

It's always lovely

to watch your reaction

....

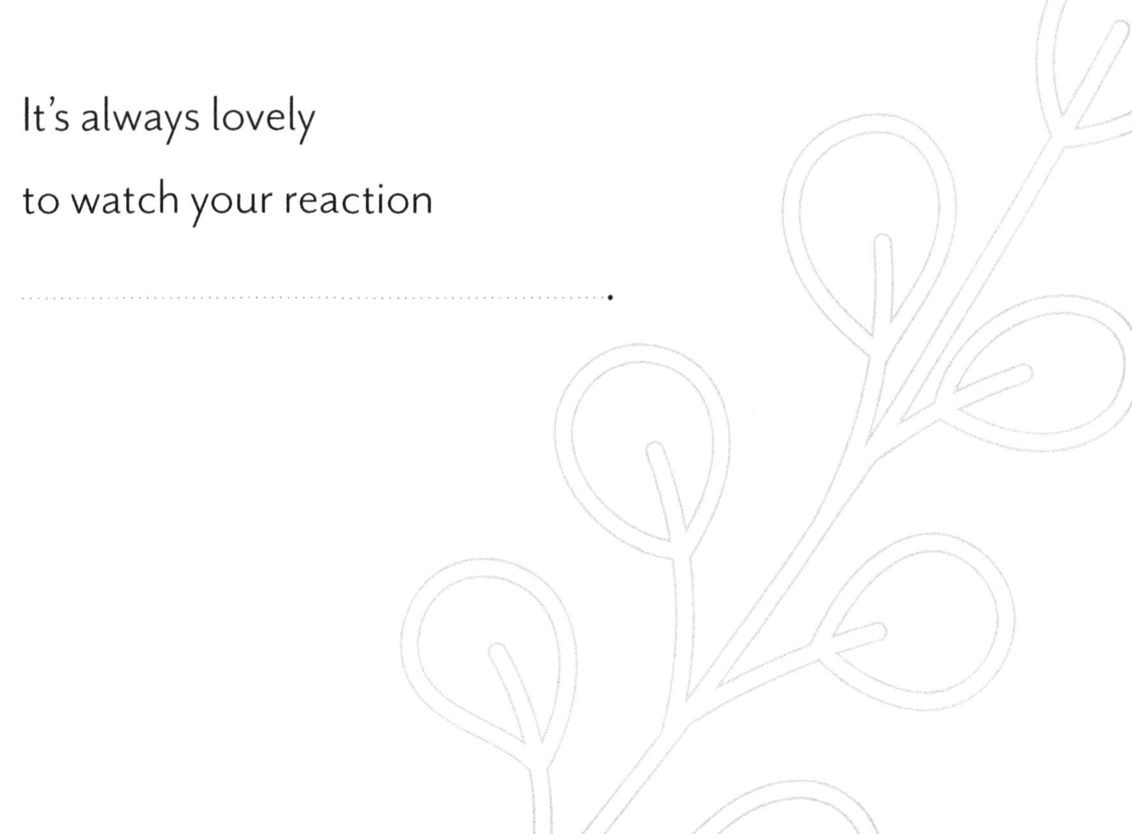

89

My absolute
favorite thing about you is

....

90

The top three feelings that I get in your presence are:

1. ....

2. ....

3. ....

91

I always loved the way you

....

when I

....

92

One thing you always do with grace is

....

93

Your ability to

....

is amazing.

94

One day, I hope to be

....

just like you.

95

You knew that I

....,

but you let it slide nonetheless.

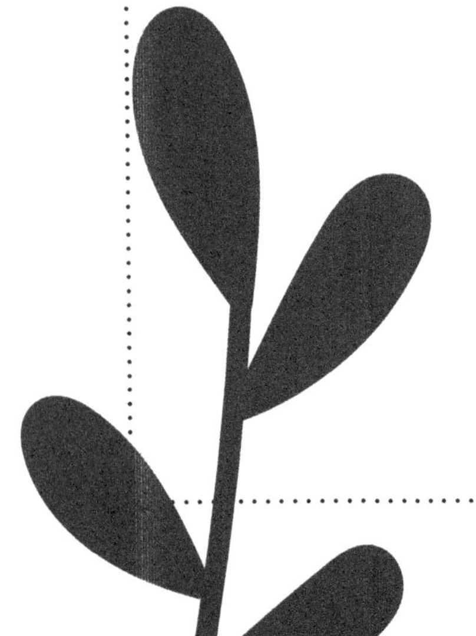

96

You raised me to be a

....

person.

97

The time when you

....

will be forever engraved on my heart.

98

You are my biggest supporter when it comes to

……………………………………………………………………….

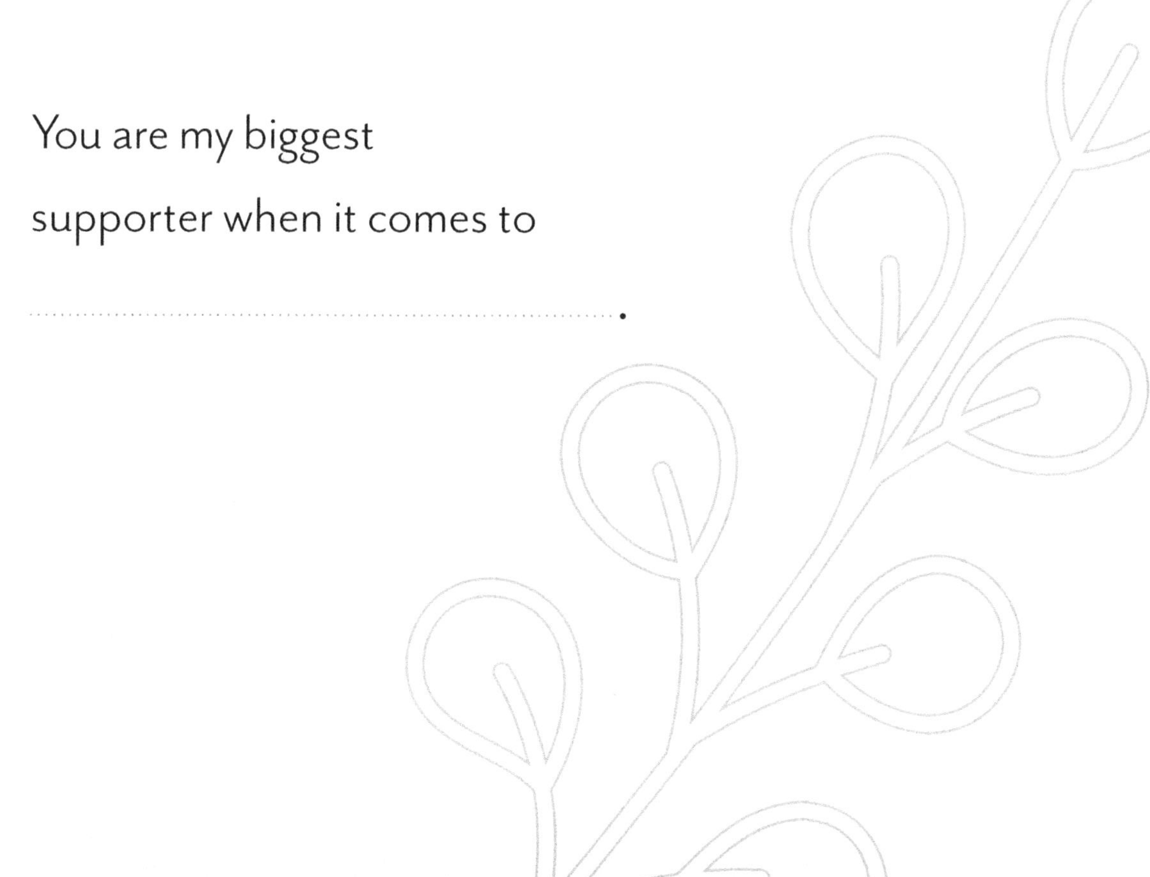

99

You introduced me to

…………………………………………………………,

and that changed my life for the better.

100

The top three things I most look forward to doing with you over the next 10 years are:

1. ....

2. ....

3. ....

The most unique thing
I love about you that sets
you apart from everyone else is

....

I love you mom!

Made in the USA
Coppell, TX
11 May 2023